HEROES OF BLACK HISTORY

MUHAMMAD ALI

BY MICHAEL RAJCZAK

Gareth Stevens
PUBLISHING

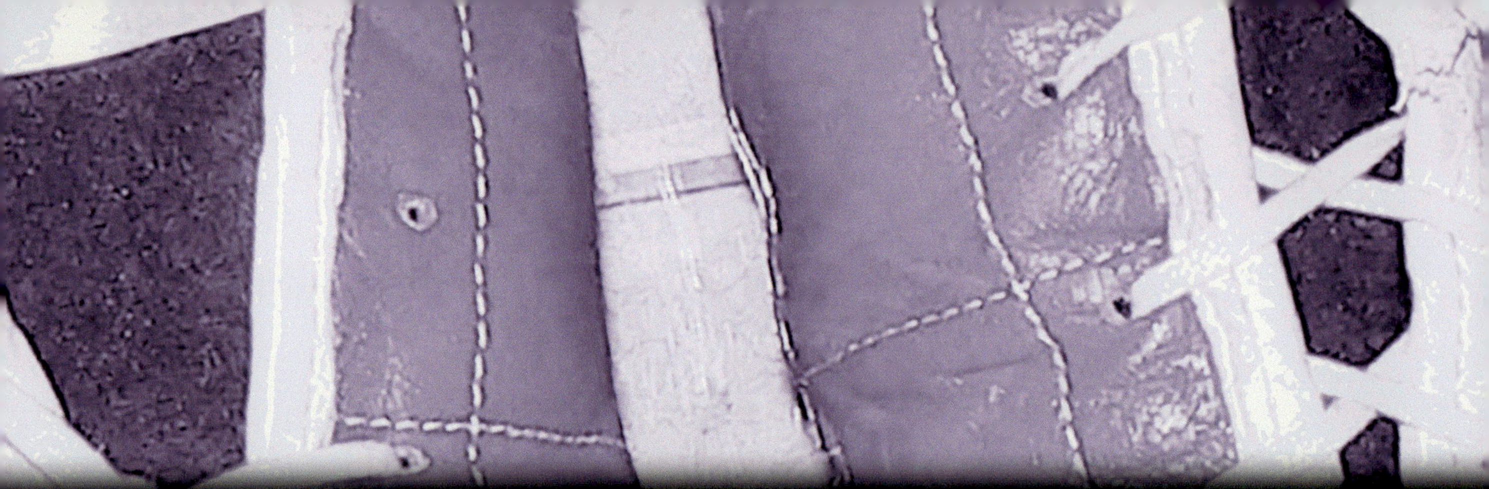

Please visit our website, www.garethstevens.com. For a free color catalog of all our high-quality books, call toll free 1-800-542-2595 or fax 1-877-542-2596.

Library of Congress Cataloging-in-Publication Data
Names: Rajczak, Michael, author.
Title: Muhammad Ali / Michael Rajczak.
Description: New York : Gareth Stevens Publishing, [2021] | Series: Heroes of black history | Includes bibliographical references and index. | Contents: The greatest of all time – Born Cassius Clay – The young champion – The 1960s – "The fight" – The rumble in the jungle – Three-time champion - After the ring – Legacy.
Identifiers: LCCN 2019050739 | ISBN 9781538257968 (library binding) | ISBN 9781538257944 (paperback) | ISBN 9781538257951 (6 Pack) | ISBN 9781538257975 (ebook)
Subjects: LCSH: Ali, Muhammad, 1942-2016–Juvenile literature. | African American boxers–Biography–Juvenile literature. | Boxers (Sports)–United States–Biography–Juvenile literature. | Political activists–United States–Biography–Juvenile literature.
Classification: LCC GV1132.A44 R35 2021 | DDC 796.83092 [B]–dc23
LC record available at https://lccn.loc.gov/2019050739

First Edition

Published in 2021 by
Gareth Stevens Publishing
111 East 14th Street, Suite 349
New York, NY 10003

Designer: Laura Bowen
Editor: Monika Davies

Photo credits: Cover, p. 1 (Muhammad Ali) The Stanley Weston Archive/Contributor/Archive Photos/Getty Images; cover, pp. 1–32 (background) Raul654/Wikimedia Common; p. 5 John Shearer/Contributor/The LIFE Picture Collection/Getty Images; p. 7 James.Pintar/Shutterstock.com; p. 8 Evening Standard/Stringer/Hulton Archive/Getty Images; pp. 9, 13, 15, 19 Bettmann/Contributor/Bettman/Getty Images; p. 11 Central Press/Stringer/Hulton Archive/Getty Images; p. 12 William Lovelace/Stringer/Hulton Archive/Getty Images; p. 16 U.S. Army/Handout/Hulton Archive/Getty Images; p. 17 Robert Abbott Sengstacke/Contributor/Archive Photos/Getty Images; p. 21 Focus On Sport/Contributor/Focus On Sport/Getty Images; p. 23 John Iacono/Contributor/Sports Illustrated/Getty Images; p. 25 STEPHEN JAFFE/Staff/AFP/Getty Images; p. 26 MARIA BASTONE/Staff/AFP/Getty Images; p. 27 Paula Bronstein/Staff/Getty Images North America/Getty Images.

Printed in the United States of America

CPSIA compliance information: Batch #CS20GS: For further information contact Gareth Stevens, New York, New York at 1-800-542-2595.

CONTENTS

Words in the glossary appear in **bold** type the first time they are used in the text.

THE GREATEST OF ALL TIME

In 2005, President George W. Bush presented Muhammad Ali with one of the highest honors a U.S. citizen can receive: the Presidential Medal of Freedom. This was a great honor for Muhammad Ali, especially because the famous boxer was once **convicted** by the U.S. Government for refusing to fight in a war.

Ali's life story had ups and downs. Few could argue about Ali's special talents in the boxing ring. He became perhaps the best-known boxer in history, known for his spirit and fast-footed fighting style. In this book, you will discover the incredible journey that is the life of Muhammad Ali.

A STRIKING SPIRIT

Muhammad Ali was known for his loud but sparkling personality, or set of qualities. He was proud to call himself "the greatest [boxer] of all time." His self-confidence made him a symbol of black pride. Jim Brown, a celebrated football player, once said of Ali: "He made people accept him as a man, as an equal."

Muhammad Ali had no trouble proclaiming his points of view.

BORN CASSIUS CLAY

Boxing great Muhammad Ali was born on January 17, 1942, in Louisville, Kentucky. He was the first of two sons born to Cassius Marcellus Clay Sr. and Odessa Grady Clay. His parents named him Cassius Marcellus Clay Jr. He was born at a time in the southern United States when black people often had to live separately from white people.

Cassius wasn't a very good student at school. He struggled with spelling and writing. What he did have was **determination** and a strong belief in what he could become. Instead of writing his goals down, he would doodle pictures of himself reaching a goal.

BARELY GRADUATED

Cassius Clay had a learning challenge called dyslexia, which made reading hard for him. He was barely able to graduate from high school. However, by then, his boxing achievements were well known. In fact, his high school principal **predicted** that Cassius Clay would be one of the best-known graduates of Louisville's Central High School.

This is the boyhood home of Cassius Clay, redone to look like it did in the 1950s. In this cottage, Cassius grew up with his parents and younger brother, Rudolph.

At the age of 12, Cassius and his younger brother shared a brand-new bike that cost $50. One day, when it began to rain, they parked the bike outside and ran into a building to wait out the storm. When the rain stopped, they came out to discover the bike had been stolen.

Cassius was upset about the theft. He went looking for the bike and the person who'd taken it. Finally, he found a police officer named Joe Martin. When Cassius told Joe that he would "whup" the person who took the bike, Joe suggested that Cassius learn how to fight first.

A NATURAL FIGHTER

Joe Martin was also a boxing trainer. After meeting Joe, Cassius went to train with him day after day. Cassius proved to be a natural fighter. He was very quick. After training for just six weeks, Cassius won his first boxing match. He went on to win six state Golden Glove Championships in high school.

CASSIUS AND HIS BROTHER RUDOLPH, 1963

Here, a 12-year-old Cassius strikes a boxing stance. He'd go on to win 100 of his 105 nonprofessional boxing matches.

THE YOUNG CHAMPION

At just 18 years old, Cassius took his astonishing boxing skills to the Rome Olympics in 1960. Confident and bold, Cassius defeated three more experienced fighters on his way to the gold medal match. In his final match, he faced Poland's Zbigniew Pietrzykowski. Four years earlier, Pietrzykowski had won the Olympic bronze medal.

The Polish fighter came out strong, scoring better and clearly leading the match. Cassius knew he had to be stronger in the third and final round in order to win. Cassius overpowered Pietrzykowski and had him tired against the ropes as the round ended. The judges declared Cassius the Olympic light heavyweight champion.

POOR TREATMENT

Although he was an Olympic champion, some people only saw Cassius's skin color. Restaurants in his hometown refused to serve him because he was a black man. The story goes that Cassius was so upset at this treatment he threw his gold medal into the Ohio River. However, it's now believed Cassius instead just lost the medal.

Cassius (second from right) said after the 1960 Olympics, "I didn't take that medal off for 48 hours. I even wore it to bed."

Cassius had a very different style of boxing than most professional fighters of his day. He held his hands lower, moved away from punches, and relied on his speed to avoid getting hit.

On February 25, 1964, he challenged Sonny Liston for the world title of heavyweight boxing champion. Using his quickness against a slower Liston, Cassius was able to land fast combinations of punches. Liston was getting swarmed with punches and had injured his shoulder. He could not continue after round six. Cassius came in as an underdog and left as the new heavyweight boxing champion.

REMATCH

A follow-up fight with Sonny Liston came three months later. Liston fell down in the first round. The champion stood over him, urging him to get up and fight, but Liston remained down. A ring official told the referee that Liston had been down for 20 seconds, longer than a 10 count. That ended the fight.

SONNY LISTON

If a boxer is knocked down, he has a count of 10 to get up or he loses the fight.

THE 1960s

Cassius grew up during the civil rights movement. During this time, black people fought for equal civil rights, or the freedoms granted by law. Many black people sought to address the **prejudice** against them that was part of their daily lives.

Some black people, including Cassius, became interested in the encouraging messages from the religion of Islam. Cassius decided to convert, or change his religion to another religion.

When Cassius converted to Islam, a leader suggested he take on a new name to reflect his new beliefs. Cassius Clay then became Muhammad Ali. From that point on, anyone calling him Cassius Clay would be corrected or not answered.

EQUALITY

When the civil rights movement began, black people were separated from white people in schools, restaurants, and other social situations. If a law was broken, black people often received much more severe punishments. Black people were also not allowed to live in the same neighborhoods as white people. The civil rights movement wanted equal treatment for all.

This 1964 photograph shows Cassius, who became known as Muhammad Ali, proudly displaying his world heavyweight boxing championship belt.

During the 1960s, the United States began military action that grew into the Vietnam War. Adult men in the United States were drafted to fight in this war, including Muhammad Ali. This angered him. He felt he had no quarrel with the opposing side. However, if someone receives a draft notice, the law says they have to report for service.

Ali's poor schooling at first **disqualified** him from service. The rule was changed a few years later, and Ali was required to join the army. He refused to do so for what he said were religious reasons. He was found guilty of draft **evasion** and stripped of his heavyweight title.

KEPT FROM THE RING

Muhammad Ali wasn't allowed to box for three years. During this time, he fought in court to get this decision overturned. He also made speeches opposing the war. Ali was a popular sports hero, and his refusal to go to war sent a powerful message. In June 1971, the Supreme Court overturned his charge of draft evasion.

AMERICAN SOLDIERS IN VIETNAM, 1967

The Vietnam War was a conflict starting in 1955 and ending in 1975 between South Vietnam and North Vietnam in which the United States joined with South Vietnam. Here, Ali explains to the press his decision to not fight in Vietnam.

THE FIGHT OF THE CENTURY

When Ali received permission to fight again, his goal was to get back his heavyweight championship title. Joe Frazier was now the heavyweight champion. There was a lot of anger between the two boxers. Ali bad-mouthed Frazier for years, calling him mean names at times.

Ali and Frazier were opposites in many ways, from their personalities to boxing styles. Their first fight on March 8, 1971, was nicknamed the "Fight of the Century" and considered by many to be the greatest boxing match in history. Both fighters were undefeated, and had claim to the heavyweight championship title. In the end, Frazier won the 15-round brawl.

A LEGENDARY RIVALRY

Ali and Frazier fought each other three times in total. Their rivalry—seen inside and outside the ring—has gone down in history as legendary. Ali and Frazier had a 1974 rematch in which Ali came out as the winner. The 1974 victory meant Ali went on to fight the heavyweight champion at the time: George Foreman.

Ali and Frazier fought a third time in 1975. The fight was called "The Thrilla in Manila." Muhammad won the fight. The fight was so fierce, Frazier's eyes nearly swelled shut.

THE RUMBLE IN THE JUNGLE

One of Ali's greatest moments was during "The Rumble in the Jungle." This fight took place on October 30, 1974, in Africa. Ali was set against the mighty champion, George Foreman. Foreman came into the fight undefeated in 40 fights, including 37 knockouts.

A FIGHTING CHAMPION

After the "Rumble in the Jungle," Ali defended his title 10 more times. Though a champion, many people noted that Ali seemed to be slowing down. He still had the power to finish off opponents. His last knockout was against Richard Dunn in 1976.

How could Ali beat a younger, stronger, and bigger opponent? Ali used his "rope-a-dope" method, covering up from punches with his arms while against the ropes. He **absorbed** punch after punch. This tired out Foreman—exactly what Ali had hoped for. In the eighth round, Ali began landing lightning-fast combinations of punches on the weary champion. Foreman went down and was counted out. Ali had regained the championship.

A second fight against George Foreman never happened. Twenty years later, Foreman regained the heavyweight title, becoming the oldest champion at age 45.

THREE-TIME CHAMPION

The years were catching up to Muhammad Ali. Some people quietly remarked he wasn't as fast as his younger days. In comparison, Leon Spinks was a young, promising fighter who had won Olympic gold. On February 15, 1978, he faced Ali for the heavyweight championship. Spinks was more forceful and displayed more energy than Ali. Spinks won a 15-round decision on points—and the championship.

Seven months later, Ali won the championship back. Ali defeated Spinks before more than 63,000 fans in New Orleans's Superdome. The win made Ali the first boxer to win the heavyweight title three times.

FOR THE RECORD

In his 21-year-long career, Ali won 56 bouts, or matches. He won the heavyweight championship three times and only suffered five defeats, or losses. He came out of retirement to fight his friend, Larry Holmes. However, Ali was getting older and couldn't finish the fight. Later, Ali said to Holmes, "I don't know, Larry. Something was wrong with me."

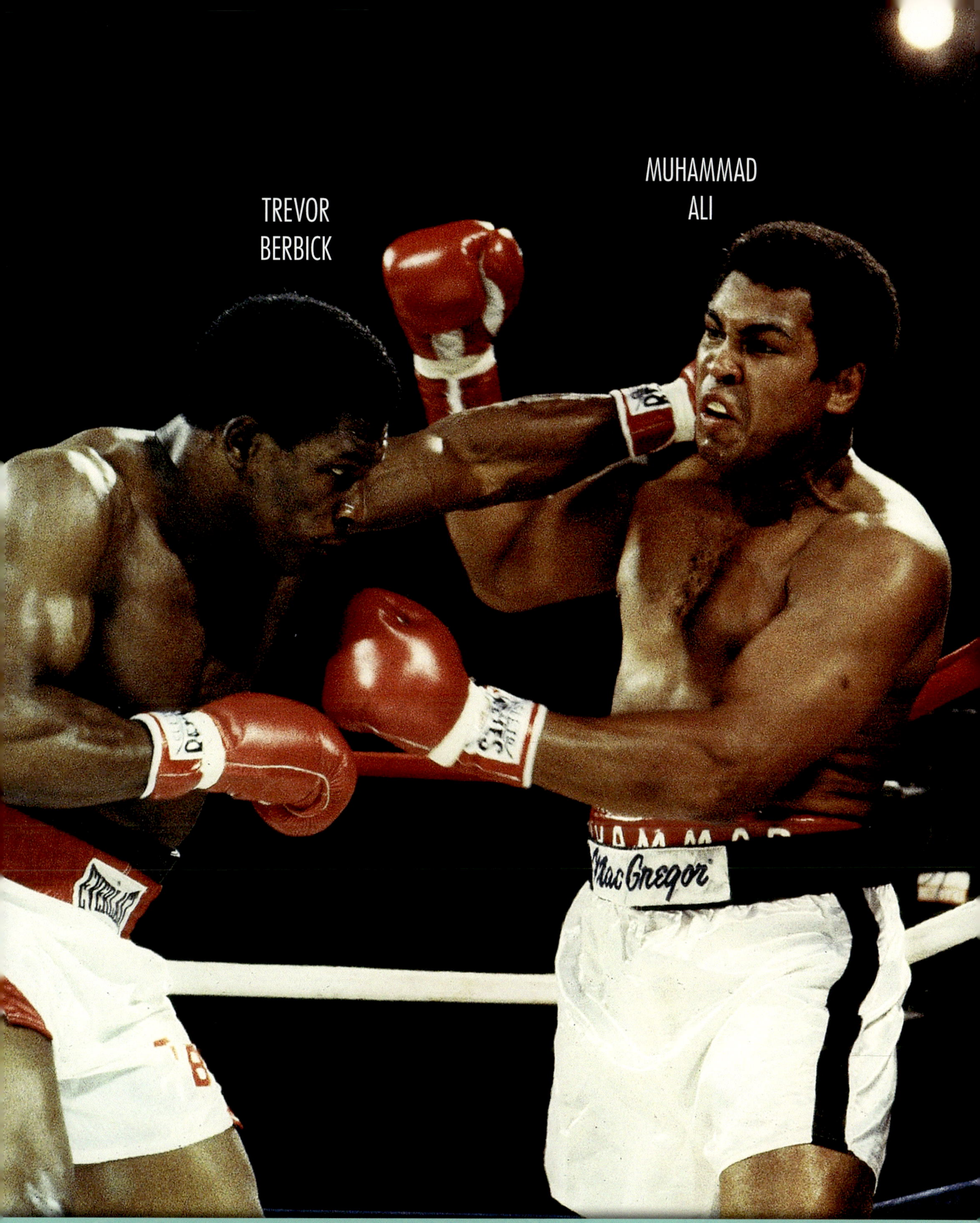

Ali had one last fight on December 11, 1981.
He lost a 10-round decision to Trevor Berbick.

AFTER THE RING

Three years after his last fight, Muhammad Ali was **diagnosed** with Parkinson's disease. This is a disease, or illness, that causes a person's muscles to grow weaker. There's currently no cure for Parkinson's disease, but there are treatments, or kinds of medicines to make living with the disease easier. The treatments address the disease's symptoms, or signs that show someone is sick.

Ali used his position as a well-known public figure to raise greater awareness and share information about Parkinson's disease. In 1997, he co-founded the Muhammad Ali Parkinson Center in Phoenix, Arizona, where doctors study the disease and treat patients.

MORE ABOUT PARKINSON'S

Parkinson's disease is a medical condition caused by the loss of nerve cells in the brain. This affects how a person moves different parts of their body. A person with Parkinson's disease finds their muscles start to slowly weaken. Their hands or head also may shake. Often people with this disease find it difficult to speak clearly.

Muhammad Ali lived with Parkinson's disease for 32 years. He's photographed here with Michael J. Fox, a well-known actor who also has Parkinson's.

Ali said he wished to be remembered as someone "who never looked down on those who looked up to him...who stood up for his beliefs...who tried to unite all humankind through faith and love." To this end, he spent a lot of time helping others.

Ali supported the Make-A-Wish Foundation and the Special Olympics. He also raised money for medical supplies and food for people in need around the world. He met with religious and political leaders to support peace and respect throughout the world. Ali even became a United Nations Messenger of Peace in 1998.

SEEKING FREEDOM

After **dictator** Saddam Hussein of Iraq captured 15 Americans to hold as hostages, Ali decided to travel to Baghdad, Iraq, to try and get them released. This was tough for him. The effects of Parkinson's disease made it very hard for him to get out of bed. After a week, the dictator met with Ali and released the hostages to him.

ALI WITH RELEASED HOSTAGES, 1990

MUHAMMAD ALI'S FAMOUS QUOTES

"Float like a butterfly,
sting like a bee."

"You don't lose if you get knocked down;
you lose if you stay down."

"Impossible is not a fact.
It's an opinion."

"Don't count the days;
make the days count."

"It isn't the mountains ahead to climb that
wear you out; it's the pebble in your shoe."

"Service to others is the rent you pay
for your room here on Earth."

ALI VISITING A SCHOOL IN AFGHANISTAN

LEGACY

Muhammad Ali was a one-of-a-kind, larger than life individual. Sportswriter Dick Schaap once said that even as a young 18-year-old, Ali was "the most alive figure I had ever met." American commentator Howard Cosell called him "the most **devastating** fighter who ever lived."

Ali once said he'd like to go down in history as "a great boxer who became a leader and a champion of his people." During the 1960s, some viewed him as a **radical** who went against his country. Today, Muhammad Ali is remembered as a person of peace who wanted to make the world a better place.

LIKE FATHER, LIKE DAUGHTER

Muhammad Ali's eighth child is Laila Ali. Muhammad Ali didn't believe boxing was a sport for women. He once asked her, "What are you going to do if you get knocked down in the ring and the whole world is watching?" Laila answered, "I'll do what you did and get back up." Laila went on to win several world boxing championships.

The Life of Muhammad Ali

JAN 17	1942	Born in Louisville, Kentucky
SEP 5	1960	Wins Olympic gold medal
FEB 25	1964	Wins first heavyweight title, knocking out Sonny Liston
MAR 8	1971	First fight against Joe Frazier known as "Fight of the Century"
OCT 30	1974	Wins second heavyweight title, knocking out George Foreman
SEP 15	1978	Wins third heavyweight title versus Leon Spinks
DEC 11	1981	Last fight
JUL 19	1996	Lights Olympic torch in Atlanta, Georgia
NOV 9	2005	Receives Presidential Medal of Freedom
NOV 19	2005	Muhammad Ali Center opens in Louisville, Kentucky
JUN 3	2016	Muhammad Ali dies at age 74

GLOSSARY

absorb: to take in

convict: to prove or show someone is guilty of a criminal act in a court of law

determination: the act of deciding something firmly

devastate: to cause widespread damage

diagnose: to identify an illness by examining someone

dictator: someone who rules a country by force

disqualify: to stop or prevent someone from being a part of something, usually for having broken a rule

evasion: the act of avoiding something

predict: to guess what will happen in the future based on facts or knowledge

prejudice: an unfair feeling of dislike for someone or a group of people because of their race, sex, religion, or other quality or feature

radical: a person with views very different from the usual, especially related to politics

FOR MORE INFORMATION

BOOKS

Buckley, James, Jr. *Who Was Muhammad Ali?* New York, NY: Penguin Workshop, 2014.

Gregory, Josh. *Muhammad Ali.* New York, NY: Children's Press, 2017.

Haskins, Jim. *Champion: The Story of Muhammad Ali.* New York, NY: Bloomsbury USA, 2018.

WEBSITES

Fight by Fight: Muhammad Ali's Legendary Career
www.usatoday.com/story/sports/2016/06/04/muhammad-ali-fight-by-fight-career/85341622/
Follow the whole boxing career of Muhammad Ali, fight by fight.

Muhammad Ali: The Ultimate Fighter
www.bbc.com/timelines/zy3hycw
Dive deep into Ali's life with this timeline.

Parkinson's Disease
kidshealth.org/en/kids/parkinson.html
Learn more about Parkinson's disease here.

Publisher's note to educators and parents: Our editors have carefully reviewed these websites to ensure that they are suitable for students. Many websites change frequently, however, and we cannot guarantee that a site's future contents will continue to meet our high standards of quality and educational value. Be advised that students should be closely supervised whenever they access the internet.

INDEX